The
Philosopher's
Daughter

LORI DESROSIERS

To Donna,

5-22-13
Cotuit MA

From one "poetry goddess"
to another,

Lori Desrosiers

salmonpoetry

Published in 2013 by
Salmon Poetry
Cliffs of Moher, County Clare, Ireland
Website: www.salmonpoetry.com
Email: info@salmonpoetry.com

ISBN 978-1-907056-98-7

COVER ARTWORK: © *Freesurf69* | *Dreamstime.com*
COVER DESIGN & TYPESETTING: *Siobhán Hutson*

Printed in Ireland by Sprint Print

Dedicated with love to my beautiful mother Blanche, who gave me my first journal and who always told me I was a writer.

Deep love and thanks to my beloved husband Gary and my gorgeous and talented daughters, Margot and Gabrielle for your continuing love and encouragement. Thank you also to my wonderful friends in Deep Dish Poets and CB's for your honest critique and support.

Also, to the memory of my father, Leonard Charles Feldstein, who encouraged me to see the world with wonderment.

Acknowledgements

"That Pomegranate Shine" won the Greater Brockton Society for Poetry and the Arts 2010 poetry contest for New England Poets. X.J. Kennedy judged.

"That Pomegranate Shine" also appeared in the *International Journal of Psychoanalysis'* blog.

"Conducting in Thin Air" and "Twinkle" appeared in *New Verse News.*

"Thinking Rock" appeared in *The Smoking Poet.*

"Hudson" appeared in *BigCityLit.*

"The World is Flat" appeared in *Shape of a Box.*

"Some Answers" and "Reverie Obscura" appeared in *Chickenpinata.*

"Redhead at the Miss Flo" appeared in *The Equinox.*

"Mother's Tongue," "The Room at the House in Croton," "Mile Swim," "Closer to God," "Mother's City," "Womanly Ways," "Blanche Remembers," "Last First Kiss," "Mother's Tongue," "The Broken Doll," "Mom at Sixteen," "If, Mother," "From the Porch," "Grandmother's Hands," "Hudson," and "Girls 1970" in *Three Vanities*, chapbook, Pudding House Press 2009.

"Neon S_ns" and "Clyde" appeared in U.M.Ph. Prose Journal.

"Les Cigales" appeared in *Pirene's Fountain* and *The New Millenium Anthology* (finalist).

"Wrestling with the Poem" appeared in *Clattery Wrestling Anthology.*

"Looking at Bees" appeared in *Tygerburning.*

"Grandmother's Hands" in *Modern Jewish American Poets* Anthology.

Contents

Daughter's Places

Internal Spaces

Starting Places

(June 11, 2009) – In an unfortunate twist of fate, a woman who missed the Air France flight that crashed into the Atlantic last week has been killed in a car accident. – (AP)

Conducting in Thin Air

When someone on high waves
his or her baton, is that that?
Is your symphony over,
your song sung, are you done, *finis*, *kaput*,
even if by some trick of Karma
you missed the flight that crashed?

Or is it just a strange coincidence,
these folks who bumbled through their lives,
forgetting where they put their keys,
dropping pens, spending too much
time with friends, lingering
too long in conversation,
enjoying the music a bit too much,
like my dad used to when he drove,
conducting Beethoven in thin air,
my mother shouting, "Len, *please*,
keep your hands on the wheel!"

Thinking Rock

Small girl steps on moss,
wades through wild hyssop.
In the woods she is safe
from pernicious imaginary monsters.
Into green glen, to the thinking rock,
an alluvial formation, flat topped.
She climbs to the top, sits,
thinks until she is tired of thinking.
In Summer warmed by sun,
in Winter a monument to frigidity,
still a place to trudge to,
leave tracks leading
to the jangle of bells on doorknob,
calling her back to the house.
When her grandfather is there,
she watches him smoke his cheroot,
have a whisky with her father.
Smoke rings rise like grey ropes.

Hastings-on-Hudson

for Jon

Waves lap the river bank beneath
"Heaven and Earth" in stone by Lipschitz.
We walk the narrow shoreline
beside soot-blackened tracks of
Metro North commuter rails.
At sunset, bats darken sand to black.
We pick up the pace, though these
flying mice hunger for mosquitoes, not children.
Our sneakers leave indents
beneath the canopy of willow trees.

Last Seat, Second Violins

In 7th grade, Mr. Hayden would throw his baton
at anyone who played a wrong note.
Small hands trembled, eyes squinted,
trying to decipher Stravinsky.
Little pencil notations,
finger numbers over treble clefs.
Orchestra practice began 7:50 sharp.
Leaving bikes outside, we shuffled in,
black cases swinging,
tabs slung open,
rosin swiped back and forth
over horsehair bows,
tightened just enough to sing.

It was easy to "fake bow"
follow the notations, gliding
above the string, no one
could hear our silent symphony.
Melody carried by first chairs,
high school girls, braces off,
dyed blond hair,
full breasts heaving below
chin rests, red nails on bows.
Practicing "The Firebird Suite"
in my room at home,
fingers high on the E-string, fifth position,
made my mother ask,
"Do you have to do that
when we're here?"

My violin sits in the closet now,
bridge broken,
rosin in crumbled fragments.
But the case still smells like early mornings,
holding it, I feel the bruise under my chin.

The Room at the House in Croton

Stucco walls to trace small fingers over,
lacy bedclothes, white sheets
smelled of bleach and sweat,
maple furniture with pink knobs,
drawers brimming with sun-dried clothing,
fresh from the line, then starched
with spray on Mother's ironing board.

Shaped like a piano,
music box opened,
played Brahms' lullaby.
A ballerina turned on red felt,
folded down when closed.
Record player in the corner
scratched out thirty-threes.
My brother and I danced
on oak floors.

Treasure chest overflowing
with dress-up clothes.
We were princess and cowboy,
china tea set, beaded necklaces and dolls—
Porcelain faces with shiny blue eyes
that opened and closed, with lashes,
their dresses and tiny black shoes with
straps littering the round white rug.

Little brother, fresh from his bath,
wrapped in white terry towel
dragged through my neatly
arranged tea party, tipping
the Chatty Kathy, making her moan,
teddy bears rolling around on the
floor—running from me, trailing
wet footprints out the door..

Mile Swim

Twelve years old, I stand in blue summer-stained one-piece,
wait alongside fellow campers' goose-bumped bodies
to start the swim across lake Coniston,
rowboats and canoes ready in case we should drown.
We plunge into icy water, crawl away from the screaming
children on shore, relieved it is not their turn today.

The mile swim—final ritual of Red Cross course.
Our toes brush lake muck, seaweed, fishes,
shadowy spirits of unhappy campers forced to swim on rainy days,
shadows of early morning polar bear clubbers.
Pass wooden docks, knee scrapers, splinter makers,
concerned counselors in their tight white caps.
We hear the tap-tapping of oars,
soft splash of other arms/ feet kicking.

Out past the others, my strokes are strong.
To my surprise, I am alone.
Blue ripples, cloudless sky,
silence smells of dragonflies.
At the center of the emerald lake
all is green-gold and shimmery.

For a moment I am free—
free from swimming lessons,
the endless teasing,
the pain of my budding breasts,
my parents' divorce.

When the others catch up.
We swim to shore.

A Dog's Day

That day we visited our father, sick with brain cancer,
he was barely able to speak.

We walked with him in the woods,
his yellow mutt Hector bounding alongside.

My brother and I each held a hand,
helping to steady his gait.

After the visit, we got in the car, argued,
then joked to numb the pain.

During our walk, Dad was able to say a few words,
"Nobody loves me except Hector".

Looking at Bees

Among the rushes on the shore
the only bright thing
was a bee's black and yellow abdomen

Three trials
one of bees, one of bicycle, one of whirlpool
the year I turned six

At the sight of bees
I tried to hold myself
as still as the moon

I don't usually enjoy
the sound of buzzing
but today the mower
sounds like home
although the bees
seem annoyed

It was the bees' fault
hiding in deep woods brush
I almost died

Running up the hill
covered with welts
ladies offering jars
of various bright hues
Daddy would have
something that
wouldn't hurt

He rode up the drive
in his magic coach
with a doctor's bag
and a hug for me
his baby girl.

The night
when we counted
the bee stings
there were
fifty-two

Neon S_ns

In 1961, the year I learned to read,
my parents took me on the bus
down Madison Avenue, past the park,
across 34th Street to 8th Avenue,
and through Times Square.

It was early evening, but the neon
signs already flashed full tilt.
I read "Girls, Girls, Girls,"
"Adults only" and "XXX".
"What does X,X,X spell?"
I asked. No answer came.

Small town lights still blink
"Coca Cola," or an incomplete
name of a diner proclaims "Miss"
without naming the girl,
or "The _____ tel" leaves us in the dark,
wondering what was meant.

Above the highway, an abandoned
sign flashes only one letter, "R."
In the window of the tailor's shop,
the last person in town to sew a hem,
the sign flashes "Custom __wing."

In the Croton Woods 1965

Boulder in forest clearing,
my brother and I stood on top
shouting, "I am the king of the hill!"
Diggers of worm piles,
denizens of deer trails,
builders of birch bark shacks,
wanderers under warbler nests,
exciting birds with our pounding feet,
disturbing puddles, sand on dry days,
climbing trees, kicking fallen apples,
corduroy pants ripped on sticks
brandished in fake fencing.

Dolls were dragged outdoors,
dressed in maple leaf tunics,
their hair twisted with dandelion stems.
Heads popped off, then stuck back on.
Barbie barely survived
her trip downstream
tied to a bottle of Prell.

'59 Olds

I'm six, gripping the seat of my father's '59 Olds
as we make our way up the winding Croton Hills.
"Sit back!" Mother shouts at every turn.
Eyes closed, I still know where we are.

Tumble to the right, round the big curve
by the High School, then sharp left
(knock into door handle) as we begin the climb
up the hill, past the funeral home, the skating pond.

Our steep driveway throws me on my back, feet in air.
I am the first female astronaut on her way to the Moon;
blasting off in her jalopy/spaceship, its engine drowning
out next year's divorce, my father's early death.
The Olds grinds to a halt; our ship has landed.
My father opens the door.

Girls 1970

My best friend used to
hook her little finger around mine.
We would take the train into the City,
walk around the West Village,
shop for beads and baubles.

Elbows kissed,
arm around the other's waist.
A man at the bodega
said we looked like
we just stepped off the boat:
kerchiefs tied behind long auburn hair,
matching denim skirts swung like bells,
narrow ankles tucked in Chinese shoes.

Cross-legged on her quilt-covered bed,
we beaded headbands on a small loom,
or embroidered our bell-bottom jeans.
Oh, the intoxication of secrets,
of unrestrained giggles,
how we let the boys
touch us everywhere but *there*.

Vaginas safely tucked
under layers of Carter's and slips,
white upon white,
under denim, under patches,
"…where does the time go?"

Paris 1950

Footsteps on cobblestone
Blanche eats crêpes on Ile de la Cité
learns to sing Schubert.
Leonard studies philosophy
at the Sorbonne
(Trout, pancake, Spinoza)
I am only a thought.

Closer to God

My father used to say,
"Children are closer to God."
When I was very small
before there were words
coursing through my mind,
there were sunbeams
filtering through my nursery window.
I recall the songs of sparrows,
the clang of milk delivery,
horses' hooves on cobblestone,
the smell of burning chestnuts,
my mother humming lullabies,
my father's exultant laugh.
He died at 63,
mute from brain cancer.
In his last moments
did he reclaim this wordless awe?

Star-Cancer

Professor of Philosophy and
author of three books on Metaphysics,
my father died of an astrocytoma,
a brain glioma with star-shaped cells.

At first, his sentences came backwards.
Doctors removed one tumor,
then star cells embraced his spinal cord.

Radiation singed his imagination
and ours, its heat, directed solar flares,
unsuccessful.

Star-cancer took my father
faster than a red dwarf swell,
sudden as a super-nova burst.

Big Words

Pulling my father's Philosophy book up on Google,
I read the dedication to his many friends and the part
where he calls his children pure and

the future generation and hopes that we will
live according to our own ideals, which I try to do
now that I am nearly as old as he was when he died.

The cancer took his language first
those beautiful big words he used every day.
In fact, when I was little he taught me words

like "symbolic" and "essential." At age four or five
he'd ask me to tell his friends what I learned today,
and he would be bursting with delight that I

actually understood and could use vocabulary.
But to me it was a game and I matched his joy
with mine, anything to spend time with him.

I would learn a thousand big words
If they could bring him back.

Mother's Places

last first kiss

He was a violinist,
told her
he would pay
for voice lessons.
She described him as
older (27) and going bald.
She was seventeen
when this rich man
asked her to marry him.
She said no,
she had already been kissed
by my father,
who had no money,
but at eighteen
had long lashes,
blue eyes—
and silky blond hair.

Mother's City

Bell toll of A-line skirt called like Pavlov,
"Look at me, look at me"
below my young mother's tightly belted waist,
arms crossed above bountiful hips.
Whistles trailed behind high heels,
clicking on pavement like tiny drumbeats.

I ran along behind, careful not to mess my
light blue dress with the pearl buttons;
the one I fought not to let her throw away,
so she gave in, and hung it on my closet door
for more than a year after I outgrew it.

The city understood my mother.
It was large, and gritty, like her imagination.
Escape to theater or opera always
just a cab-ride away, not like Croton,
where she and my father began fighting.

Pristine country home, painfully gorgeous,
Mother foundered five years under
tulip trees, ivy vines and clover, until,
overcome with longing, returned.

I listened for imaginary bombs
as we hid under desks,
protection, perhaps,
against nuclear calamity,
but no shelter whatsoever
from divorce.

womanly ways

my mother taught me
the womanly way:

to pull up stockings:
roll one down, then roll it up

to brush long hair:
stroke gently, starting at the ends

to sit with a skirt:
close legs, carefully crossed at ankles

to keep things neat:
have a big drawer to hide the mess

to fix things:
marry a man who is handy

to bring up happy children:
have plenty of handkerchiefs, and a piano

to make peace:
apologize, even if you're right

Blanche Remembers

In 1933 in Chicago,
they would see
gangsters in classic limousines,
the ones with rounded fenders.

Dillinger and his gang
were shooting up the town.
Her brothers played
cops and robbers,
or stickball;
ran wild in the streets,

In the tiny apartment.
she had no bed
slept on a trunk.

She and her brothers
got scarlet fever.
Their mother was sick too,
so the kids had to go
to different hospitals.

She wrote to her brother,
"My hospital has cute mice.
What is yours like?"

He wrote her back,
"Please don't send
any more letters.
You are a bad girl
telling lies about mice."

He never believed her.
Even now,
at eighty-six
he thinks she was lying.

Mother's Tongue

Her silk voice sang Brahms Lullaby,
rocked her babies,
cradled us so long ago,
protected us like the half-moons
of wooden rocker feet.

Her sharp voice
stopped tiny hands
from irons, fire, filth.
Warned us away
from traffic and strange men.

Her scream
clashed with my young voice,
accompanied,
the one time I swore at her,
by a slap in the face.

I could never out-sing her,
she was too strong.

Lately, her voice quavers with age.
We squabble over time.
She wants mine,
my grown daughters'.
But their voices are strong.
I haven't the power
over them she has over me

The Broken Doll

They even sold her dolls.
Nothing left but to flee
Philadelphia for Chicago
a chance for her father to work,
a chance to start again.

Just one dolly, Blanche pleaded,
pennies were saved, months passed.
Oh, a beautiful doll, with lashes,
a pink dress and long blond curls!

It was too much for five-year-old Sol.
He was the baby, wanted the attention,
took the doll from the top shelf of the closet,
and ripped her to shreds.

At sixteen, Sol worked Atlantic City's
Million Dollar Pier, won ten dolls,
and gave them to his sister,
who accepted them grudgingly.

When I asked Blanche, now 84,
"did that make up for what he did?"
she said, "Not really."

Mom at Sixteen

Smooth flesh not yet kissed,
Dark curls not yet gray,
Cracks in sienna photograph.

Lipstick deeply red,
intense slate eyes,
same as your granddaughter's.

Before you worked at Woolworth's
instead of going to college,
before you married Dad.

Your smile is sly, sexy, tough.
Still a girl, there's fight in you.
Before you gave up singing:
your "woman's sacrifice."

Before the divorce,
the sixties, feminism, Vietnam.
Not yet cursed with diabetes, children.

Before you helped us, time after time.
Always open-handed, hearted, strong—
also vain.

You are wearing a white dress
(perhaps it is pink) with puffed sleeves.
You stare straight ahead, unafraid,
at your future.

Grandmother's Hands

Grandmother's hands, veined, soft
petticoats she sewed floated white
on clothes line blowing far aloft
gathered on her arm for the night

petticoats she sewed floated white
by Ukraine's river long ago
gathered on her arm for the night
a man her family would not know

by Ukraine's river long ago
long brown curls, green eyes glowing
a man her family would not know
gathered her up, skirts blowing

long brown curls, green eyes glowing,
grasped the ship's rail as wind's gust
gathered her up, skirts blowing
sad to leave, but knew she must

children's laundry gently tossed
on clothes line blowing far aloft
gathered clothespins, none were lost
Grandmother's hands, veined, soft

No Wind

You're so thin
if you stood alone
the wind would take you.

Your hands are still beautiful
tucked into starched sheets.

Now one of mine
encases yours completely.

I remember holding your pinky
walking New York sidewalks,

your high heels ticking,
my little feet trying to keep up.

Sometimes, your hands
would swoop down,

lift me through the air
into a perfect hug.

No wind could take us then.

If, Mother…

Remember in Paris,
how we turned the wrong way
onto the Boulevard Saint-Michel?
How calm you were,
veered off the boulevard,
cars honking,
angry Frenchmen swearing.
A few minutes later
I could see your heart was beating fast.
We both exhaled and cried, astonished
how close, that day, we came to death.

When your tongue is quiet,
there will be no more stories:
No more trips to 1930's Chicago,
no languid afternoons
on Margate beach,
no Cape Cod Bay,
No looking into your lovely face—
buckets swinging,
foam against black rocks—
to see my own loveliness.

Daughter's Places

From the Porch

Work-weary, I settle into wooden rocker
Maples flutter, yellow summer wind.
Retired couple strolls by softly talking.
Crickets audible over car noise.
Mailman in blue shorts drops another book.
Trash cans wait patiently.
A rift of jet smoke splits the sky,
buzzing louder than the neighbor's mower.
Mark, my friend's boy, is over there.
He writes the countryside in Iraq is lovely,
but soldiers leave trash by the side of the road...
perfect place to hide a bomb.
She comes by and helps me garden.
The hyacinths we planted are white and blue.
The gladiolas bloomed this week, blood red.

Spirit Birds

You found the place
where they were nesting.

Blue heron:
descendants of the Egyptian phoenix,
steady flyers, rulers of all fish
according to the Hitchiti tribe,
Creek people whose name means
"to look upstream."

Blue-gray wings
reach to the horizon.
Your kayak reaches them
only when the water's high,
then you can travel
to gaze upon the Benu birds.

But the water recedes
so fast there is no time
for stories.
The herons take off,
wings dripping,
fish in beaks.

Hudson

My river, you run brimming
with barges, tugboats, trout.
Flanked by Catskills and Palisades,
your source is Lake Tear of the Clouds,
Adirondack mountain stream.
Your Mohican name is *Muh-he-kun-ne-tuk*.

Trout breech into ever
widening circles. Heron and egret
wade in the shallows, eagerly fishing.
At sunset, bats rush from shoreline caves
catching mosquitoes in mid-air.

Ancient oak trees lean,
gesticulating toward the opposite bank,
their roots touching the shallows.
The shadows of great bridges,
George Washington, Tappan Zee,
ripple your waves on a windy day.

The World is Flat

A boy I know
drove off a cliff
following the GPS in his car.
GPS systems think
the world is flat
no mountains, valleys or
boulders, no cliffs,
no ups or downs,
just left and right,
east, west, north, south.

I found an old friend
on Facebook.
She emailed me twice.
We hadn't talked in
thirty years—
still haven't.
Computers think
the world is flat.
I stare at the screen
and wonder if there
are any real people
out there.

My students text
instead of talk,
even sitting
side by side.
I make them buy books.
They buy online,

never visit the bookstore—
They go to the library
because I take them.

Cell phones
reduce literature
to one letter symbols
like u and r.
Cell phones don't
study philosophy,
but u should try 2
figure out who u r.

Wedding

Marvelous planner, you were:
perfectly styled hair, lace gown, antique rings,
two little girls to hold your train.

His hair, his suit, his smile just right,
his children gave out flowers.
Everyone is smiling in the pictures.

…if you could just go back and tell yourself to run.

Some Answers

Lord, Lord, can you believe it?

The way you water the ferns.

Minor chord on a piano resolves to major C.

Where the icicles used to hang.

The coat hooks on the wall are not even.

Trains backed into engine houses, ready to start out again.

Painted flypaper unstuck.

The way you look at me sometimes.

Bridges crumble in your eyes.

Cold and blue with drips of water rushing into grates.

Still haven't forgiven myself
for leaving you at the pizza place.

There were eight of us,
five children, three adults
in two vehicles and we each
thought you were with
the other one, but nevertheless

how could I have done this—
gotten all the way home before
noticing you were missing?
I rushed back across town

to find you tearful, surrounded
by the waitresses,
trying to get you to eat some pizza,
but at four years old your eyes told me
you understood very well what had happened.

Train Ride in Winter

Trestles and tunnels,
rumbling by bridges,
arched over rivers,
funnels of smokestacks.
Strange cranes
lifting silver pipes,
past a park lit by lanterns
looks last century.
Benches by fences
waves on a river,
a line of sunshine
follows us forward.
Gnarled tree limbs,
branches arranged
against ice islands.
Fields of frost
reveal stalks of
some sort of plants.
The forest thickens,
we expect to see
deer or rabbit but
it is empty.
Past brick buildings,
an outdoor bathtub.
What sort of people
leave laundry on the line
on a balcony in winter?
Apartments on a river
with hundreds of windows,
the bank so steep they

should fall in the water.
Long lines of cars
backed up at a crossing,
graffitied school bus
full of children
waits as we roll by.
Between two factories
a forgotten pond.
Flock of ducks lands,
in pale blue water
ripples behind them.
I am completely happy.

AOL Health News:
(Oct. 1) - Doctors in India are baffled as to why a young girl spontaneously bleeds through her pores without being cut or scratched. Twinkle Dwivedi, 13, sometimes wakes up in the morning covered in dried blood that has seeped through her eyes, nose, hairline, neck and the soles of her feet. She has undergone several transfusions.

Twinkle

Mystics and Krishna won't cure you
India's child of bleeding pores
in blue and fuscia striped pajamas
waiting for another transfusion
another doctor to say he doesn't know.

Mother asks the Sufis
to sing and dance for you
al *hamdu'l 'illah* but nothing happens
your face is lovely I see why they
called you Twinkle and the red stain
runs down your cheek like a teardrop.

You try to smile
for the cameras hoping someone will
bring the right medicine
poor little star
so the children will play with you again
so the Sufis will go sing for someone else.

Redhead at the Miss Flo

The black-eyed waiter
brings me a black and white menu.
There is a redhead seated alone.
I take a wobbly stool two down.
In the red booths the wrinkled lady
with curled glasses gums her meatloaf.
The construction guy with the earring
and the other one with the hat
slurp the soup of the day,
tyrannosaurus rex with noodles.
The waiter leans over,
kisses the redhead on the cheek.
She opens her
pink painted mouth and speaks.
Her voice is shrill, sounds like she looks.
"Is there bread pudding today?"
"Yes, want some?" She pouts.
"No, I don't want any. Give me a refill."
He pours the root beer into her white plastic cup.
The straw stands up as he drums on the counter,
disturbing salt and pepper shakers.

The diner is a tin can.
My hunger has led me to peel it open,
to walk across the black and white squares of linoleum,
worn by the boots and shoes of years of customers,
munching fish and chip specials,
cramming cole slaw into their mouths,
scuffed by a hundred heels of waltzing waitresses
slipping mayonnaise-laden tuna salads onto plates
busing piles of limp French fries
to the kitchen behind the counter,
leaned on by locals for years and years,
stained by the water rings of a thousand plastic cups.

Between Rounds

ugly tattoos
spattered
with the other guy's blood

chewing on mouth guards
leaning on ropes
cornered at the
edge of the world

coaches shout
and cauterize
arteries pound
behind battered ears

mighty leg muscles
twitch anxiously
meat against meat

when the bell sounds
fate hangs
on a count
of ten

The River Keeper

Jane with the blue eyes
rowed her boat in Storm King's shadow.
Below, dark water,
an incalculable depth.
Above, an immensity of sky.
Setting her jaw,
she pounded her oars against the current.

She knew the shores,
the mountains' trails on both banks,
the tulip, maple and elm trees,
how to navigate the rapids,
where to step,
which rushes to grab
to pull the boat ashore.

Her people are the river keepers,
guardians of Croton Point,
of the World's End above Peekskill,
where ships must slow
above an underwater mountain.
The Hudson is hers,
child of Seeger's songs and
Boyle's Dutchmen, of Mohawks
and Irving's headless horseman.

Jane no longer takes her boat
out on the river.
Her legs are arthritic,
her rowing arms weak.
Yet, she still pounds her oars
against the current,
the river's light reflected
in her blue eyes.

That Pomegranate Shine

*Two brides arise from the river, shivering and shining
like pomegranate seeds.*

—WORDS FROM AN ARMENIAN SONG

I was the wrong kind of bride,
more sweat than glisten,
more peach than pomegranate.
At twenty-three, in love with marriage,
not the man,
I plunged into rough water,
bringing grandmother's candlesticks,
mother's books and two silver trays.
Ten years later, I emerged shivering,
dragging my ragged volumes,
one candlestick and two babies.
On the bank, I shook off the water
and breathed.
Standing with my children,
looking out over the river,
the new brides asked me where
I got that pomegranate shine.

Room with Feathers

My daughter wears a wide-brimmed
black-feathered hat, veil intact,
her full-red lips grin, peek out
beneath the trim. Pink boa hangs

on hook-fettered wall, beside
a painting of a rooster, purses,
a shawl the color of peacock plumes.
Her room, though modest,

is well-preened. Unlike at my house,
here she likes to clean.
Dresses from Salvation Army
only slightly worn, still gleam.

Room with feathers manifests her art.
Eiderdown's the measure of her heart.

Internal Spaces

Reverie Obscura

I am on a bus,
the mountain road, precipitous,
a silver bridge stretches over
churning water below, no railings.
The bus stops, we get out.
I am with a man, perhaps a lover.

The water is gone, now
there is a desert below,
cactus in bloom, green lizards skitter.
I can see for miles.
Sky painting dissolves to fuscia.

Then we are on a train, going backwards.
The world goes by upside down,
a camera obscura, light peeks
through pinhole windows
reflecting on black walls.

We sit upside down
to see the world right side up.
"This is poetry," he says,
and I am falling now,
falling out of the poem.

Wrestling with the Poem

We pose opposite one another
like Hercules and the Cretan Bull,
but the mad beast gets away from me again,
terrorizing the lands beyond my desk,
here in Massachusetts, not in Greece.
Some days I try to sneak up on him, guerilla style,
but he dances away,
snorting at my inadequacies.
Despite my study of poetics,
my piece of paper on the wall,
the innocuous M.F.A.,
a two year's journey into conversation,
followed by workshops with the best of poets,
a few good sparks, perhaps a flame,
the match continues.
We fall together.
When I find a hold,
the poem slithers out, that oily boy.
So, I look for a new move,
try a poem a day, a practice,
in thirty days a few good possibilities.
Now there are thirty new bulls
wrestling me to the ground.

Les Cigales (The Cicadas)

"Les cigales, les cigalons, chantent mieux que les violons".
LES CIGALES—Gerard, French Art song

After sixteen years underground the bugs
emerge, their butter brown wings sticky,
climb the nearest tree to dry and harden.
They lay their eggs in wet green oak leaves,
then sing for days and days until the singing
lifts them up to swarm and die, crashing
blindly into fences, trees and homes,
before their larvae creep down trunks of trees
to find a place below the ground,
and wait another sixteen years.

At sixteen a girl is emerging
from years beneath her mother's skirts.
Her butter brown eyes dewy, her gaze
not yet hardened. She lies down
beneath the oak, weeps and weeps until
the rain begins to fall, then runs inside
the house, her room door crashing shut.
She crawls beneath the bed, a place
to wait until a first lost love disperses
among the evening song of the cicadas.

What Poets Do Instead of Sleep

When I think of my poet friends,
I think of them swimming naked
in a pool of words,
their skin porous,

finding just the right ones
to put in secret pockets and take out at midnight.
We hold open our hands,
catch the dropping metaphors

as they slide off desks onto the floor.
We are all awake,
juggling synonyms in the air,
pulling verbs from jars with pitchfork pens,

letting adjectives, adverbs and articles pile up
in wastebaskets and cabinet drawers.
We clip *ings* off gerunds with the long scissors,
pin nouns to the wall letting them dry to a crisp.

We string sounds together with twine,
then hang them out in the night air,
for we know poems age better
hidden from the sun.

Clyde

You know, he had a hungry look.
Entering the Blue Goose Diner,
you couldn't miss the man.
Such girth could only mean
there would be a big tip.

He was in and out of tune:
harmonica hung from his belt
a tease below the belly not yet full.

He spent hours messing with songs.
Sometimes one would sound just right,
like the steak and onions on the menu
he ordered every Thursday.

Mary used to cook for him Saturdays.
As he spun her around the kitchen,
her skirts waved, fanned the air,
making it sweet.

The bingo girls called him
from the booth in the corner.
He told them if they weren't careful
he'd have to come over there.

Then one Thursday in July
he didn't come in.

Mary and her new boyfriend came;
Johnny the cook, and the waitresses too.
After the funeral, they
talked about how badly
he played the blues.

Call

I could stand on the edge of a chasm
colored like the Grand Canyon, orange
in sunlight, blue as the sky darkens,
call your name, hear the echoes
resounding back to me off the cliffs,
just the way they do at home,
when I call out silently in breath,
on the road beneath the car's hum,
or when I am alone. Only then does
your name curl before me in air
invisible to all but me. A high whine,
Coyote creeps the canyon, makes
me think it is you responding,
in the azure haze of every evening.

Transformation

Evening shadows stretch.
Rooftops are grey cathedrals,
pigeons become pterodactyl.

Alleyways amplify—
each door's a thunderclap,
every creak's a scream.

Spirit locomotive rumbles down
Main Street, blowing its double wail,
dragging the dark like a gypsy caboose.

Drunk

In daylight she diverts her gaze,
tries to pretend it's not happening.
When he says he can stop
any time, no problem,
she wants to believe him.

Night hangs overhead,
an acrid wind chokes
and won't let go.
He is on his tenth beer
or so.

His words slur and she cleans
as if to stave off Death,
His four furious horses galloping in,
just around the bend,
sweating, foaming at their bits.

Night Writing

" ah, the desire, ah, the writing…"
—ANNE WALDMAN

Writing past midnight as usual
I enter a poem with one idea,
end up writing another.
You are already asleep for hours.

I lie down beside you, reach out.
You hold my hand for a while,
then fall back to sleep, snoring.

My breasts are round as similes,
each nipple an exclamation point,
vagina warm as a slant rhyme,
my hands and fingers are verbs.

I come quietly beside you,
a flutter of breeze, a small wave.

My body freed of words,
your breath lulls me to sleep.

LORI DESROSIERS' chapbook of poetry, *Three Vanities*, a chronicle of three generations of women in her family, was published by Pudding House Press in 2009. Her poem "That Pomegranate Shine" won the Greater Brockton Society for Poetry and the Arts award in 2010. Her poetry has been published in *New Millenium Anthology* (finalist), *BigCityLit*, *The Smoking Poet*, *Concise Delights*, *Blue Fifth Review*, *Ballard Street Poetry Journal*, *Common Ground Review*, *Meat for Tea*, *Pirene's Fountain* and many others. She publishes *Naugatuck River Review*, a journal of narrative poetry. She earned her M.F.A. in Poetry from New England College in New Hampshire She also sings and had a CD of original music published in 1998. When not working, running around to poetry events or editing, she enjoys eating good food, having stimulating discussions, and dancing.